IN MY
FOOTSTEPS
A Traveler's Guide to
MARTHA'S VINEYARD

Christopher Setterlund

Schiffer Publishing Ltd

4880 Lower Valley Road • Atglen, PA 19310

Other Schiffer Books by the Author:
In My Footsteps: A Cape Cod Travel Guide, 978-0-7643-4209-7

Other Schiffer Books on Related Subjects:
101 Things to Do in Martha's Vineyard, Gary Sikorski, 978-0-7643-4953-9
Martha's Vineyard Perspectives, Arthur P. Richmond, 978-0-7643-3834-2
In Every Season: Memories of Martha's Vineyard, Phyllis Méras, 978-0-7643-4095-6

Published by Schiffer Publishing, Ltd.
4880 Lower Valley Road
Atglen, PA 19310
Phone: (610) 593-1777; Fax: (610) 593-2002
E-mail: Info@schifferbooks.com

Cover design by John Cheek
Type set in BauerBodni BT/Helvetica Neue LT Pro
ISBN: 978-0-7643-5019-1
Printed in China

All photographs © Christopher Setterlund

For our complete selection of fine books on this and related subjects, please visit our website at www.schifferbooks.com. You may also write for a free catalog.

Schiffer Publishing's titles are available at special discounts for bulk purchases for sales promotions or premiums. Special editions, including personalized covers, corporate imprints, and excerpts can be created in large quantities for special needs. For more information, contact the publisher.

We are always looking for people to write books on new and related subjects. If you have an idea for a book, please contact us at proposals@schifferbooks.com.

CONTENTS

INTRODUCTION

"Martha's Vineyard is a place like no other—miles of unfettered coastline and natural beauty, delicious locally sourced food, a vibrant arts and culture scene, and one-of-a-kind shopping make the island a must-go destination!"

– Nancy Gardella, Executive Director, Martha's Vineyard Chamber of Commerce

Martha's Vineyard was first spotted by Bartholomew Gosnold in 1602 on his expedition from England to the New World. Gosnold most likely named the island after his daughter Martha, or possibly after his mother-in-law Martha Goulding, who contributed funds for said expedition. The "vineyard" part of the name is for the vines that covered the island when explorers first landed. Before Gosnold arrived, the native Wampanoag tribe called the land *Noepe*, meaning "middle of the waters." The first written mention of Martha's Vineyard comes in English writer William Strachey's manuscript about the first Virginia colony, *The Historie of Travaile Into Virginia Britannia* in 1610.

The Vineyard's closest-to-land tip is roughly three miles away as the crow flies from Cape Cod, and today the island is an easy forty-five minute ferry ride from Woods Hole, Massachusetts. At about 96 square miles, Martha's Vineyard is the third largest island on the East Coast of the United States, behind only Long Island, New York, and Mount Desert Island, Maine. Shaped roughly like a triangle, it's about twenty-five miles long at its widest point east to west and nine miles from north to south,

Martha's Vineyard is made up of six unique towns and many smaller villages. An immensely popular vacation destination and a year-round home for an increasing number of people in the past few decades, the island is enjoyed by everyone from presidents and celebrities to everyday working people.

Rich in history, culture, and natural beauty, the island is also still home to the Wampanoag Tribe, a sovereign tribal nation centered in the town of Aquinnah.

Step aboard a ferry, or fly in from the mainland, and prepare for all the wonders The Vineyard has to offer.

GETTING THERE

Take a ferry from Woods Hole or Hyannis on the Cape, or fly in via Cape Air, either from Hyannis or one of the other airports that the airline serves. (Seasonal flights are also available on Jet Blue and Delta from JFK in New York and on US Airways from DCA in Washington, DC.)

THE STEAMSHIP AUTHORITY
1 Cowdry Road, Woods Hole

The Steamship Authority was established in 1960 and is the only ferry service to the islands that carries both passengers and vehicles. The terminal in Woods Hole on Cape Cod sits within sight of the Vineyard and can bring visitors to the island in about forty-five minutes. There are two ports on the Vineyard where the Steamship Authority docks, in Oak Bluffs and Vineyard Haven, though the Oak Bluffs port is in use only from May through October. The ferries are amazingly proficient at on-time deliveries with delays only occasionally caused by the weather. Schedules and fares change with the seasons and are available on their website: SteamshipAuthority.com. (**GPS:** 41.522873, -70.670209)

> The Steamship Authority provides safe, convenient, and reliable transportation to island residents and visitors. As the lifeline to the island, we offer the lowest fares, free wireless Internet on vessels and at terminals, year-round service and daily departures for passengers, automobiles, and trucks. Come aboard the *Steamship Authority* . . .it's the way to go to Martha's Vineyard!
> —*Kimberlee McHugh, Director of Marketing, The Steamship Authority*

HY-LINE CRUISES
220 Ocean Street, Hyannis

This company's roots go back to when it was called Hyannis Harbor Tours in 1962. Hy-Line got its name in 1972 when Hyannis Harbor Tours bought out Nantucket Boat Company. Not only has Hy-Line been running ferries to both Martha's Vineyard and Nantucket for decades but in 1988–89 they introduced first-class ferry travel as well. Hy-Line offers 55-minute high-speed ferries to Martha's Vineyard from their docks in Hyannis on Cape Cod. They also offer seasonal ferries in between Martha's Vineyard and Nantucket. This inter-island service is incredibly convenient for those who wish to see both islands before returning to the mainland. (**GPS**: 41.647907, -70.279305)

CAPE AIR

660 Barnstable Road, Hyannis

If the idea of a ferry ride seems too long, or if you are coming from far away, a small but exceptional airline serves the island. In 1989 Cape Air was founded by current CEO Dan Wolf as a single route, three flights daily between Provincetown and Boston. Today there are flights all over the United States and even to some Caribbean Islands. The majority of their planes are small Cessna 402s carrying a maximum of nine passengers. It is a quick and very safe way to hop from Barnstable Municipal Airport in Cape Cod over to Martha's Vineyard's Airport, which is centrally located on the island. (**GPS:** 41.669225, -70.292279)

II

OAK BLUFFS

After arriving at the dock in Oak Bluffs (**GPS:** 41.458341, -70.554956), the next step is choosing a way to get around on the island. If you brought your own vehicle then please proceed to the first location. If you came without one you are in luck. There are a few ways to navigate the Vineyard once you arrive. Here are two of them.

For convenience and affordability this is a great option. The VTA, as it's known, provides year-round transit to all six Vineyard towns. During the peak season of May through October there are fourteen routes that take travelers all over the island. In addition to one-time rides from town to town, there are also passes ranging from one-day, seven-day, and thirty-one day, all the way up to an annual pass. The VTA has a stop only a few hundred feet from the Steamship Authority dock so you can step off the ferry and onto the shuttle and be on your way after you walk your way through Oak Bluffs.

ANDERSON'S BIKE RENTALS
Circuit Avenue Ext.

For those wishing to explore the Vineyard while enjoying the elements as well, there is the option of renting a bicycle. Anderson's is a quarter mile from the Steamship Authority dock—about

a five minute walk. They have been in business since 1971 and have a great knowledge not only of which bike is right for each person but also about the Vineyard in general. Their prices are very reasonable. You'll get a lock, helmet and map, and the shop provides roadside assistance while you are out and about. The prices and models are subject to change, and a visit to their website is recommended. AndersonsBikeRentals.com

Now that your mode of transportation has been chosen, it is time to see Martha's Vineyard, starting in Oak Bluffs and heading west around the island. These directions will begin from the ferry dock and will try to lead you around in geographical order to make the most of your time.

GPS: 41.45688,-70.556066
Directions: From the Steamship Authority ferry dock turn left onto Seaview Avenue. It is 0.1 mile to the first destination.

1. OCEAN PARK
Seaview Ave., Oak Bluffs

The beautiful bandstand is visible before one even steps off the ferry. The seven-acre Ocean Park is the very first site welcoming you to Oak Bluffs. The bustle of the ferry dock seems miles away though the park is only a few hundred yards away. Across the street from Inkwell Beach, the park is a slice of flat green land perfect for playing Frisbee or simply sitting on a bench and watching the gaggles of geese drink at the man-made pond.

The park is surrounded by beautiful Victorian homes on Ocean Avenue, some with unique looks and colors to them. The bandstand was built in 1887 by the Martha's Vineyard Club to hold a twenty-five piece band.

GPS: 41.454872, -70.557064

Directions from Previous Site: From Ocean Park continue along Ocean Avenue for 0.2 miles to the next destination. (Distance: 0.2 miles Driving Time: 1 min.)

2. DR. HARRISON TUCKER COTTAGE

61 Ocean Ave., Oak Bluffs

Just steps from the ferry and among the outskirts of the famous "gingerbread cottages" of the Martha's Vineyard Camp Meeting Association (MVCMA) sits this Victorian gem. It is one of the largest houses of the group as it is actually two smaller structures that were joined together through an addition in the 1870s. Dr. Harrison Tucker's home played host to many large gatherings in its heyday with dignitaries such as President Ulysses S. Grant staying there.

Tucker was one of the premier residents of Oak Bluffs in its early days. He made his money through patent medicine manufacturing and helped turn Oak Bluffs from a summer resort called Cottage City into a bustling year-round community.

GPS: 41.453025, -70.555124

Directions from Previous Site: From the cottage, continue on Ocean Avenue, turn right onto Seaview Avenue. Take the third right onto Pequot Avenue. The next destination is a few hundred feet on the right. (Distance: 0.3 miles; Driving Time: 1 min.)

3. PEQUOT HOTEL

19 Pequot Ave., Oak Bluffs

This gem is steps from the gingerbread cottages of the MVCMA. It has thirty-two rooms, a spacious front porch, and it combines island tradition with modern amenities. The Pequot has been a tremendous place to stay for visitors for more than seventy-five years. It is just a short walk to all of the attractions in town.

GPS: 41.457390, -70.557124

Directions from Previous Site: From the hotel, take the first right onto Waban Avenue and then the first right onto Narragansett Avenue. Turn left onto Seaview Avenue, follow it 0.3 miles, turn left onto Oak Bluffs Avenue. The next destination is on the left. (Distance: 0.5 miles; Driving Time: 2 mins.)

4. FLYING HORSES CAROUSEL
15 Oak Bluffs Ave., Oak Bluffs

This is one arcade where adults and children can both enjoy themselves. The Flying Horses Carousel is the oldest operating platform carousel in the United States. The carousel originated at Coney Island in New York in 1876 and was moved to Oak Bluffs in 1884. The rest of the building is delightfully retro with arcade games, popcorn, and sodas. It is new enough that the kids will enjoy it, yet retro enough that adults will feel like kids again.

GPS: 41.456636, -70.557242)

Directions from Previous Site: From the carousel, continue left on Oak Bluffs Avenue, which becomes Circuit Avenue. Follow it 0.2 miles, turn left onto Samoset Avenue, and then take the first left onto Kennebec Avenue. The next destination is 0.2 miles up on the right. (Distance: 0.4 miles; Driving Time: 2 mins.)

5. 20BYNINE

16 Kennebec Ave., Oak Bluffs

This bar near the center of Oak Bluffs was established in 2014. The group that created 20ByNine has more than fifty combined years in the business and their experience shows in their beers and delicious menu. Much time and effort has been put into choosing and creating the proper beers and whiskeys for this small location. The owners' dedication to craftsmanship, quality, and community is apparent as soon as one enters the front door. It is sure to be a popular spot in town for many years to come.

GPS: 41.456119, -70.557754

Directions from Previous Site: From the bar, the next destination is back a few hundred feet on the left side, Post Office Square. (Distance: 250 feet; Driving Time: <1 min.)

6. MV GOURMET CAFÉ & BAKERY/BACK DOOR DONUTS

5 Post Office Square, Oak Bluffs

The best and worst kept secret in Oak Bluffs is this double-sided business. During the day, it is a delicious bakery specializing in items like scones, cannoli, pies, and wedding cakes. However come back around 7:30 pm, and go to the back door for a one-of-a-kind experience. Fresh and hot donuts are sold literally out of the back door of the bakery.

Opened in 2001, the bakery—both front and back doors—is open from mid-April through late-October and is well worth the rave reviews it gets far and wide.

GPS: 41.455962,-70.557537

Directions from Previous Site: From the bakery, the next destination is diagonally across the street.

7. OFFSHORE ALE CO.

30 Kennebec Ave., Oak Bluffs

A combination restaurant and brewery, Offshore Ale is a *Martha's Vineyard Magazine* Best of the Vineyard winner and a must-go spot in Oak Bluffs. For almost twenty years, this casual dining establishment is the only brewery on Martha's Vineyard, and they have a variety of creative and tasty handcrafted beers that need to be sampled. In addition to the beer, there are many delicious menu items including wood-fire pizzas that can be enjoyed inside or out on the patio.

GPS: 41.454638, -70.558166

Directions from Previous Site: From the restaurant take the first right onto David Healy Way, turn right onto Ocean Avenue, then take the first right onto Grove Avenue. Follow it 0.1 miles. The next destination is on your right. (Distance: 0.2 miles; Driving Time: 1 min.)

8. UNION CHAPEL
55 Narragansett Ave., Oak Bluffs

In the gingerbread cottage neighborhood of Oak Bluffs stands this beautiful, one-of-a-kind piece of architecture. This Victorian-style chapel has an octagon shape, making it stand out among the other buildings in the area. Built in 1870, this spot is tremendously popular for weddings and concerts, among other events. It is known for wonderful acoustics and a beautiful light inside thanks to the stained- glass windows. It is stunning inside and out, while also close to the center of Oak Bluffs. This is a great spot to visit for anyone who loves beautiful architecture and unique buildings.

GPS: 41.454453, -70.559183

Directions from Previous Site: From the chapel continue on Grove Avenue, turn right onto Pequot Avenue, take the first right onto Circuit Avenue, the next destination is on the left. (Distance: 500 ft.; Driving Time: <1 min.)

9. THE SWEET LIFE CAFÉ
63 Circuit Ave., Oak Bluffs

A fine dining powerhouse in the heart of Oak Bluffs, this spot is enjoyed by everyone from locals to presidents. This dinner-only restaurant is a regular stop for the Obama family during their Vineyard vacations and has gained quite a bit of national exposure. However, those on the island have known and raved about it for a long time. Within the past couple of years, the restaurant has come under new management and there are a few small changes and updates. The outdoor seating is incredible and in the summer lets visitors enjoy their meal while fully experiencing the vibe of Oak Bluffs after dark. The food can be a little pricey but it's well worth it to have a magical night here.

10. SLICE OF LIFE CAFÉ
50 Circuit Ave., Oak Bluffs

Tucked among the crowd of amazing shops and restaurants on Circuit Avenue is this little gem. Home to some of the best chocolate chip cookies one will find Slice of Life is a multiple *Best of the Vineyard* award winner. They serve breakfast, lunch, and dinner with options to sit out on their porch and enjoy a delicious meal while people watching.

GPS: 41.456939, -70.560198

Directions from Previous Site: From the café, head back south on Circuit Avenue and take the first left onto Samoset Avenue and then the first left onto Kennebec Avenue. Follow it 0.3 miles, turn left onto Oak Bluffs Avenue, then follow it 0.2 miles to the next destination on the left. (Distance: 0.5 miles; Driving Time: 2 mins.)

11. WESLEY HOTEL
70 Lake Ave., Oak Bluffs

On the northern periphery of the famed MVCMA gingerbread cottages sits this last of a line of historic Oak Bluffs hotels. The Wesley has been in business since 1879, and its Victorian appearance hearkens back to a bygone generation. Across the street from Oak Bluffs Harbor, this hotel currently has ninety-five rooms. The Wesley name comes from French Canadian chef Augusten Goupee who upon opening the hotel changed his name to Augustus Wesley to make a connection to the founder of the Methodist religion John Wesley.

GPS: 41.455304,-70.56143

Directions from Previous Site: From the hotel, take the first left onto Dukes County Avenue, take the first left onto Pawtucket Avenue, and then the first left onto Commonwealth Avenue. Bear right onto County Avenue, continue onto Wesleyan Grove, right onto Chapel Lane, and then right onto Trinity Park. The next destinations are all around. (Distance: 0.4 miles; Driving Time: 3 mins.)

12. MARTHA'S VINEYARD CAMP MEETING ASSOCIATION (WESLEYAN GROVE), TRINITY PARK TABERNACLE AND TRINITY METHODIST CHURCH

A few steps from the coastline sits a fairytale world. It is a thirty-four acre plot of land dotted with sublimely colored gingerbread-style cottages. There are just over 300 cottages, most built right after the Civil War. Some of these are available for rent. Originally the grounds were for religious "camp meetings" with people living in tents for the week or so that the meetings lasted. MVCMA rapidly became one of the largest such camp meeting sites in the country going from nine society tents in 1835 up to a maximum of 570 in 1868.

In the center of this other world is the Trinity Park Tabernacle. This is a wonderful piece of architecture, built in 1879 as an open-air spiritual center for the MVCMA. Martha's Vineyard High School has its graduation ceremonies here every June. It can seat up to 4,000 people and has been lovingly restored over the past several years.

The Trinity Methodist Church established in 1878 sits just to the north of the Trinity Park Tabernacle. It is still open for worship services and is another piece of the amazing puzzle that is the MVCMA. The construction of this wooden building severely cut into the funds of the MVCMA. Only a year later, the wrought-iron Tabernacle was built upon proposal of campgrounder J.W. Hoyt for less than it cost to build the church.

To walk through the tightly laid streets is to take a journey into another time and place without leaving the comforts of the island. It is almost like walking through a children's storybook.

Directions from Previous Site: From the MVCMA, head out on Pawtucket Avenue, turn right onto Dukes County Avenue, and then left onto Lake Avenue. Take the first right onto E. Chop Drive, then follow it 0.3 miles to the next destination on the right. (Distance: 0.6 miles; Driving Time: 3 min.)

13. EAST CHOP BEACH
E. Chop Drive, Oak Bluffs

On the northern side of Oak Bluffs Harbor is this small beach that many visitors pass by. Access to it is through the Oak Bluffs Yacht Club, and once on the sand there is a great view of Nantucket Sound and in the summer an endless parade of boats come in and out of the harbor. The jetty reaching out into the water is a great spot for fishing and also a little more secluded from the beachgoers. From the jetty, you can hear the chatter from the bars and restaurants across the harbor yet still seem so far away from it all. There is little in the way of parking so there is no parking fee, and there are restrooms available in season.

GPS: 41.470105,-70.567589

Directions from Previous Site: From East Chop Beach continue on E. Chop Drive, follow it 0.7 miles to the next destination on the right. (Distance: 0.7 miles; Driving Time: 2 mins.)

14. EAST CHOP LIGHTHOUSE
229 E. Chop Dr., Oak Bluffs

Not very far from where the ferry docks in Oak Bluffs, East Chop Light is so close yet feels so far away from the bustling town. Stoic East Chop Light on Telegraph Hill is in an area known as the Vineyard Highlands. Originally the hill contained a semaphore station, a precursor to the electric telegraph, thus the Telegraph Hill name. The "chop" in East Chop is an old English term meaning the entrance to a channel.

The first lighthouse on the spot was built in 1869 by merchant marine Capt. Silas Daggett and was privately owned. The current structure was erected in 1878. It overlooks Vineyard Sound with tremendous views of incoming boats as the lighthouse's lantern is seventy-nine feet above sea level. It was saved from destruction in the 1980's when ownership of the lighthouse was transferred after petition to VERI (Vineyard Environmental Research Institute).

III

VINEYARD HAVEN

GPS: 41.456196, -70.589599
Directions from Previous Site: From East Chop Lighthouse, continue south on East Chop Drive, follow it 0.7 miles, turn right onto Temahigan Avenue, then after 0.3 miles turn right onto Eastville Avenue. This becomes Beach Road. Follow it 0.6 miles to the next destination on the left. (Distance: 1.7 miles; Driving Time: 5 mins.)

1. LAGOON POND & DRAWBRIDGE

Beach Road, Vineyard Haven

This popular fishing and boating area begins at a drawbridge. It is a narrow finger of water flowing south to the freshwater Upper Lagoon Pond. There are more than 500 acres of prime fishing waters here with the best fishing occurring early in summer. This particular parking area is great for boat launching; there are several other parking areas around the pond.

Lagoon Pond is the border between Oak Bluffs and Vineyard Haven. There is a temporary drawbridge linking the two towns that was opened in 2010. A permanent bridge is being constructed with a target date of July 2016 for its completion. This current bridge has a bike path that runs along the left side making it accessible for drivers, riders, and walkers alike.

GPS: 41.453183, -70.599864

Directions from Previous Site: From Lagoon Pond. continue on Beach Road for 0.6 miles to the next destination on the left. (Distance: 0.6 miles; Driving Time: 1 min.)

2. ART CLIFF DINER

39 Beach Road, Vineyard Haven

This small diner is one of the most popular spots to eat on the entire island and for good reason. It is small but cozy with creative and delicious breakfasts and lunches. The diner gets its name from two men, Art and Cliff, who purchased it in 1943. It is currently owned by Gina Stanley, and there is even an Art Cliff Food Truck that travels around the island. This is a highly recommended stop. Note that parking is at a premium here; the lot is routinely full.

GPS: 41.453788, -70.602536

Directions from Previous Site: From the diner, continue on Beach Road, the take the first left onto Beach Street. The next destination is immediately on your right. (Distance: 0.1 miles; Driving Time: 1 min.)

3. JIRAH LUCE HOUSE (RITTER HOUSE)
Beach Street, Vineyard Haven

The history inside the walls of this home is rich. Jirah Luce built this residence in 1797. Its second owner was respected physician Rufus Spaulding, who lived here until around 1812. Spaulding was also a postmaster, justice of the peace, politician, and innkeeper. In fact, Spaulding ran the house as an inn for a time. It was inherited by his daughter Sophronia.

The home is known as one of the few buildings to escape unscathed from a great fire that swept through the center of Vineyard Haven in 1883. Over time, the home has been reported to have been a tavern and eventually a library and post office. Tisbury School principal Henry Ritter became owner of the house in the early 1900s and his family owned it until it was purchased by the Martha's Vineyard Historical Preservation Society in 1976.

4. MANSION HOUSE INN ON MARTHA'S VINEYARD

9 Main Street, Vineyard Haven

On the corner of the beautiful Main Street in Vineyard Haven is this terrific hotel with a wondrous view. The Inn also includes a health club and spa. Established in 1791, it was completely rebuilt in 2003 after a fire destroyed the hotel. The painstaking task was lovingly taken on by the owners, and it retains the original charm of the old inn.

The main attraction here might be the amazing panoramic view of Vineyard Haven Harbor from the cupola. There are tables and chairs up there so one can enjoy a drink or a bite to eat while watching the boats come and go.

5. OWEN PARK BEACH
Owen Park Way, Vineyard Haven

This spot is named for recording pioneer William Barry Owen. In 1899, Owen bought the rights to Victor Talking Machine, which became known as the Victrola, an early phonograph. He would go on to manage the London branch of the *Victor Talking Machine Company.*

The park has a tremendous view of the vessels coming into the Steamship Authority terminal. The beach itself is somewhat sheltered by a breakwater out in the harbor protecting the many boats. It is a quaint little side step from the main shopping areas of Vineyard Haven.

GPS: 41.480602,-70.600035

Directions from Previous Site: From Owen Park Beach, continue north on Main Street, then follow it 1.7 miles to the next destination on the right. (Distance: 1.8 miles; Driving Time: 7 mins.)

6. WEST CHOP LIGHTHOUSE

Main Street, Tisbury

Nestled in a quiet rural area of Tisbury is this tremendous lighthouse. It sits on Coast Guard property and is best viewed from behind the picket fence. The current structure, the second at the location, was built in 1891. This lighthouse, as with many, has been moved back from eroding cliffs. West Chop was moved in 1848 and 1891. West Chop used to have its own ZIP code and seasonal post office but they were discontinued due to USPS cutbacks.

U.S. Department of Homeland Security
**United States
Coast Guard**
West Chop Lighthouse

7. WEST CHOP CLUB OVERLOOK
Main Street, Vineyard Haven

Don't blink or you might miss this tiny little turnoff with a gigantic view. There are a few benches that provide you a front row seat for an amazing panorama of the view all the way to Falmouth on Cape Cod. The lush West Chop Club lies behind you and a long pier stretches out into the ocean below the cliffs. It is a nice spot to take a breath and enjoy a moment of serenity before continuing on your way.

8. WEST CHOP CLUB
Iroquois Ave., Vineyard Haven

Within sight of the cliffs at West Chop is a beautiful private tennis club. While this high-class site is not for all, there is a piece of history within reach along the road. The "Chop Shop," as it's known, is a gift shop and also a post office from late June through Labor Day. The building was constructed in 1892 as a post office and is named the Bangs House for the family who served as postmasters from 1932 to 1977. It is worth a second look when passing by.

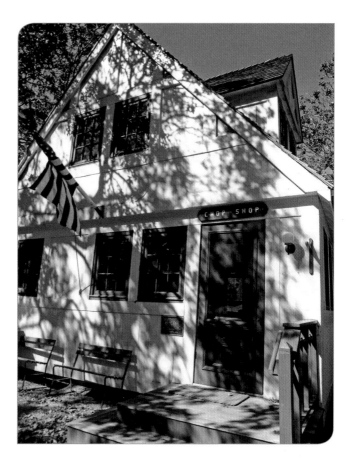

GPS: 41.449247, -70.612377

Directions from Previous Site: From the West Chop Club, take the first right onto Franklin Street, follow it 1.8 miles, turn right onto Center Street. Take the second left onto Look Street, follow it 0.2 miles turn right onto State Road. Follow it 0.3 miles to the next destination on the left. (Distance: 2.5 miles; Driving Time: 10 mins.)

9. TUCK & HOLAND METAL SCULPTORS

275 State Road, Vineyard Haven

Amazing artistic and creative ability are on display here. It was originally founded by Travis Tuck in 1974. He got his start when his first weathervane was used as a prop in *Jaws;* his shark weathervane was on top of Quint's shack. Ironically director Steven Spielberg had an original piece commissioned through *Tuck & Holand* as well, coming full-circle. Just before his passing in 2002 Tuck formed *Tuck & Holand* with longtime collaborator Anthony Holand to ensure the business would continue to flourish.

The continuation of Tuck's vision and his dedication and ability are obvious in Holand's handcrafted projects. People as far away as New Zealand have ordered his weathervanes, and there is a two-year waiting list. They were named America's Premier Weathervane Maker by *Conde Nast Traveler.*

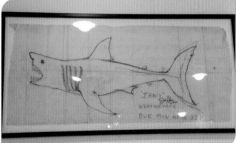

IV

WEST TISBURY

GPS: 41.433949,-70.657776

Directions from Previous Site: From Tuck & Holand continue on State Road for 3.6 miles, turn right onto Lamberts Cove Road, follow it 1.2 miles and turn right onto Manaquayak Road Continue 0.6 miles to the next destination. (Distance: 5.3 miles; Driving Time: 16 mins.)

1. LAMBERT'S COVE INN, FARM & RESTAURANT

90 Manaquayak Road, West Tisbury

Nestled deep in the woods near Lambert's Cove, this spot is worth the drive. In 1790, just a farmhouse stood on this land. Now, the Lambert's Cove Inn is popular for weddings and other formal gatherings and the property encompasses more than seven acres. Guests can enjoy tennis, a spa, many nooks and crannies to quietly hide away, and a short walk to Lambert's Cove Private Beach. The inn recently began using previously unoccupied land for a garden and raising chickens—thus the "farm" part of the name.

GPS: 41.397652, -70.677035

Directions from Previous Site: From the inn, head back out Manaquayak Road, turn left onto Lamberts Cove Road, then follow it 1.2 miles back to State Road. Turn right, follow it 1.9 miles to the next destination on the right. (Distance: 3.7 miles; Driving Time: 13 mins.)

2. POLLY HILL ARBORETUM
809 State Road, West Tisbury

Stunningly manicured and beautifully laid out, Polly Hill is a magnificent place to enjoy nature and learn a thing or two at the same time. Established in 1998 as the dream of horticulturalist Mary Louisa "Polly" Hill, this land is twenty acres of personally cultivated trees, plants, and flowers with another forty acres set aside as a nature preserve. There are many rare plants growing along the grounds that are not native to the Vineyard. Labels share some of the vital information about them.

The land the arboretum stands on was purchased by Henry Luce in 1687 and remained in his family for 200 years. The main office is actually the renovated homestead of the Luce family dating back to the mid-eighteenth century. There is also the magnificent Far Barn built in 1855, which is where the gatherings at the arboretum are held. It is a great spot for quiet solitude and natural beauty whether in the summer when everything is in bloom or winter when the plants may be asleep but the landscape is still dazzling.

The grounds are open year-round sunrise to sunset with a $5 recommended donation.

GPS: 41.381997, -70.674577

Directions from Previous Site: From the arboretum, continue south on State Road for 1.2 miles to the next destination on the right. (Distance: 1.2 miles; Driving Time: 3 mins.)

3. ALLEY'S GENERAL STORE
1054 State Road, West Tisbury

A throwback to general stores of old, Alley's is a hugely popular place. In the heart of West Tisbury, it has quite possibly all one could need, from groceries to toys to hardware and everything in between. Built in 1858, this store is small and tightly packed with products lining nearly every square inch. This only adds to its charm and appeal. There is also a farm stand behind the main general store.

In its more than 150 years of existence, Alley's has become a meeting center and island tradition. It was started by local resident Nathan Mayhew after a failed gold rush trip to California. The business underwent several name changes in its first hundred years. It eventually became Alley's after longtime clerk Albion Alley who bought the business in 1946; his children gave it his name when they took it over in 1964.

GPS: 41.381410, -70.674385

Directions from Previous Site: From Alley's, the next destination is directly across the street.

4. THE FIELD GALLERY
State Road, West Tisbury

Quite simply this is an art gallery in an outdoor setting. However, the sculptures and artwork carefully laid out in the grass and among the trees makes this something closer to a dream. The gallery was established in 1970 with the displays constantly changing. Sculptor Thomas Maley created this as a unique artist co-op, and had it designed by local architect Robert Schwartz. The 1.4-acre gallery also includes a traditional indoor gallery. The Field Gallery was purchased by the town of West Tisbury in 2011 but is still run by a small dedicated staff. It is a great showcase for artists and a great way to enjoy art even for those who may not be true art aficionados.

V

CHILMARK

GPS: 41.348508, -70.709381

Directions from Previous Site: From the Field Gallery continue south on State Road; in 0.4 miles it becomes South Road. Continue for 2.7 miles to the next destination on the right. (Distance: 3.1 miles; Driving Time: 7 mins.)

1. THE GRAVE OF JOHN BELUSHI
Chilmark (Abel's Hill) Cemetery, South Road, Chilmark

One of the original Not Ready for Primetime Players, beloved comic actor John Belushi was born in Chicago but resided in the Vineyard. His final resting place sits on a rural stretch of road in Chilmark. Belushi rose to fame in the mid-1970s and starred in *Saturday Night Live* and such films as *Animal House* and *Blues Brothers* before his untimely death in 1982.

His grave became a popular gathering place for fans but was also constantly vandalized. His wife Judy then had the gravestone moved to the entrance of the cemetery so that people

could see the stone but would not desecrate the site.

This spot is also called Abel's Hill Cemetery in some places. This name comes from Wampanoag Native American Abel Wauwompuhuque. His uncle, the sachem Mittark, was the first Christian minister at the Gay Head church in the mid-1600s.

GPS: 41.339171, -70.728736

Directions from Previous Site: From the cemetery, continue on South Road for 1.4 miles then turn left onto Lucy Vincent Road. Follow it to the next destination. (Distance: 1.7 miles; Driving Time: 4 mins.)

2. LUCY VINCENT BEACH
South Road, Chilmark

One of the most spectacular beaches on the island is also one of the hardest to get to. This spot is open only to residents of Chilmark and requires a pass during the summer. There is no sign for the dirt road for the beach. The beach was named for Chilmark librarian Lucinda Vincent who served for most of the first half of the twentieth century.

Once on the sands, the beach is a feast for the eyes. Scattered along the shore are rocks left behind by receding glaciers that create a unique picturesque view. Heading east along the shore you'll find the crown jewel of Lucy Vincent Beach—the clay cliffs. These look like they came straight out of a tropical paradise yet fit right in on the Vineyard. They provide a magnificent backdrop for many photographs. For those who feel a little wild there is also a section of this beach that allows nude sunbathing.

GPS: 41.365685, -70.747043

Directions from Previous Site: From Lucy Vincent Beach, continue on South Road for one-half mile then bear right onto Menemsha Cross Road. Follow it 1 mile, bear right onto North Road, then in 0.9 miles turn left onto Trustees Lane at the Menemsha Hill sign. There is a parking area on the right and trail maps lead you to the next destination. (Distance: 3 miles; Driving Time: 8 mins.)

3. PROSPECT HILL (MENEMSHA HILLS RESERVATION)

Trustees Lane, Chilmark

In the quiet solitude of the Menemsha Hills Reservation, a 211-acre preserve, lies Peaked Hill, the second highest point on the island. The land was bought by Nathaniel Harris in the 1860s, and remained in the family until is was sold in the 1960s to the Trustees of Reservations, a group that preserves natural Massachusetts lands for public use. Prospect Hill is a half-mile from the parking area, and a beautiful hike gradually carries you uphill. The spot is purported to have received its name from an iron ore mine near the hill. It is described in the book *Letters from an American Farmer* written by J. Hector St. John de Crèvecœur in 1782. It is also noted for its role in the War of 1812 when locals marched all along the hill giving the impression of a steady march of troops to British troops on the nearby waters.

Once atop the hill the view is stunning. From 308-feet above sea level one has a panoramic view of Aquinnah and Gay Head Lighthouse to the west and the Elizabeth Islands to the north. There is a split-rail fence surrounding the overlook and a steep drop over the side through the trees. Take caution but enjoy this spectacular vista.

GPS: 41.354664,-70.757729

Directions from Previous Site: From Menemsha Hills, turn right back onto North Road, follow it 1 mile, then bear right onto Menemsha Inn Road The next destination is on the left. (Distance: 1.1 miles; Driving Time: 3 mins.)

4. MENEMSHA INN & COTTAGES

12 Menemsha Inn Road, Chilmark

This is a perfect place to stay on the western side of the island in the quaint fishing village of Menemsha. On a narrow dirt road, the twenty-five-acre property's cottages are neatly laid out as private spaces that are also part of the inn's community. There is a fabulous view of Menemsha Harbor with views of the Elizabeth Islands prominent especially on clear days. The Mainstay suite is the original home of the Menemsha Inn. It was the farmhouse owned by Edwin Thompson that he moved in 1923 to its current location at the highpoint of the inn's grounds. Both *Travel & Leisure* and *Fodor's* have recognized this spot as a top spot to stay in New England.

5. BEACH PLUM INN & RESTAURANT

50 Beach Plum Lane, Chilmark

This is a beautiful hideaway spot enjoyed by everyone from locals to presidents. The thirteen-room inn is perched on a hill in the small village of Menemsha and has been lauded by publications such as the *New York Times*. Opened in 1950, this spot was originally constructed from an 1898 shipwreck salvaged from the nearby harbor. The seven-acre property was first owned by Theresa Morse and her husband Warren. The Beach Plum is seasonal and is open from May through October. The lodging includes options such as rooms, private cottages, and homes. It is a jewel among jewels in Chilmark.

6. MENEMSHA BEACH & SWORDFISH HARPOONER SCULPTURE

Basin Road, Chilmark

The premier spot for a sunset on the island, Menemsha Beach is tucked in Vineyard Sound. The surf is gentler than on the ocean side of the island, and the views here are magnificent. Walk out onto the breakwater and look back toward the fishing shacks, and you'll be reminded of the journey of Quint's boat, the *Orca,* in *Jaws,* beginning in Menemsha Creek.

To the right of the parking lot among the beach grass stands a seventeen-foot-tall sculpture of a man harpooning a swordfish. It is an intriguing piece of art created by Jay Lagemann. It was put in its place in the sand in 1994. It is part of the magic of Menemsha.

GPS: 41.351149, -70.765315

Directions from Previous Site: From Menemsha Beach, head back down Basin Road, turn right onto North Road, and follow it to the next destination. (Distance: 0.4 miles; Driving Time: 3 mins.)

7. MENEMSHA INNER HARBOR
North Road, Chilmark

Lined with old fishing shacks, this tiny harbor is huge on charm. It will surely look familiar as the place where Quint launched the *Orca* in the movie *Jaws*. It is easy to get swept up in memories of that movie when walking along the shores of this harbor.

The oldest of the fishing shacks, known as the Alfred Vanderhoop Shack, was built around 1865. It survived the infamous hurricane of 1938 while every other structure in the inner harbor was destroyed.

These shacks are picturesque reminders of Menemsha's, and the Vineyard's, fishing heritage. They are a far cry from the lavish homes not far away, yet have much more meaning for the shacks' longtime residents.

VI

AQUINNAH

GPS: 41.338446, -70.799077

Directions from Previous Site: From Menemsha, continue on North Road for 0.6 miles, then bear right onto Menemsha Cross Road. Follow for 1 mile, turn right onto State Road. Follow it 4.1 miles to the next destination on the left. (Distance: 5.7 miles; Driving Time: 14 mins.)

1. ORANGE PEEL BAKERY
22 State Road, Aquinnah

This is a rather unassuming spot but worth stopping for along the way through Aquinnah. An authentic Wampanoag-run business, Orange Peel Bakery looks almost like a regular house. Then one notices the beehive oven outside as well as the smell of freshly baked goods. If nobody is inside the small bakery/shop, use the honor system to make change with money in a glass jar when purchasing items.

A highlight of this locale is the famed community Pizza Night that takes place every Wednesday night from June through October and Saturday nights in May and November. Bring your own toppings, and for a suggested donation of $10 (or what you can afford), your pizza will be baked right there for you. It is a tremendous community activity.

GPS: 41.348349, -70.834994

Directions from Previous Site: From the bakery, continue on State Road for 2 miles into Aquinnah Circle for the next destination. (Distance: 2 miles; Driving Time: 4 mins.)

2. GAY HEAD LIGHTHOUSE

Aquinnah Circle, Aquinnah

On the west coast of the island, Gay Head Light is one of the most beautiful and endangered sites one will find. Overlooking the Aquinnah Cliffs, this lighthouse sits perilously close to the edge of the cliffs. As of November 2014, the fifty-one foot brick tower sat less than fifty feet from the edge of the cliffs. Thankfully the funds were raised to move the historic lighthouse. In April 2015, the lighthouse was shut down and prepared to be moved. The lighthouse was to be moved roughly 190 feet from the eroding cliffs during the summer of 2015.

The land and lighthouse became known as Gay Head in the mid-seventeenth century thanks to the cliffs of gaily colored sand and clay. The first wooden lighthouse was built at the cliffs in 1799; the current lighthouse was built in 1856. The lighthouse has been tremendously important in helping steer ships away from the dangerous underwater rocks near the cliffs known as Devil's Bridge. Gay Head Light can most likely stay in its present location for the next 140 years, based on current erosion rates.

GPS: 41.348464,-70.834989
Directions from Previous Site: The cliffs can be seen from the last location.

3. AQUINNAH CLIFFS
Aquinnah Circle, Aquinnah

There are few natural sites on the Vineyard or anywhere in New England as wondrous and sacred as these clay cliffs. They are 150 feet of sediment from six glaciers, including red and white clays that the cliffs are known for. The cliffs also bear a dangerous secret, underground rocks surrounding the base of the cliffs. These are known as the Devil's Bridge based on the Native American legend of Michabo. He was a giant who in a fit of anger cast the boulders into Vineyard Sound. These rocks made a lighthouse at the area necessary.

The cliffs themselves have been in danger as many people have taken it upon themselves to remove the natural clay from the cliffs. Taking clay baths in the ocean below the cliffs was once commonplace, but now climbing of the cliffs is prohibited. It is these cliffs that originally gave the area the name Gay Head due to the gaily colored sands and clay. The Wampanoag Tribe has always referred to the land as Aquinnah, which means "high land."

4. VANDERHOOP HOMESTEAD
Aquinnah Circle, Aquinnah

Just steps from Gay Head Lighthouse and the Aquinnah Cliffs is this special place for the Wampanoag Tribe. The home was built in the 1890s by Edwin DeVries Vanderhoop after five and a half acres was purchased by his father William. Edwin was a whaling captain and the first member of the Wampanoag Tribe to sit in the state legislature. The home is now the Aquinnah Cultural Center and is also popular for weddings with its incredible view of the southern side of the Aquinnah Headlands, a vast hillside stretching all the way down to Moshup Beach.

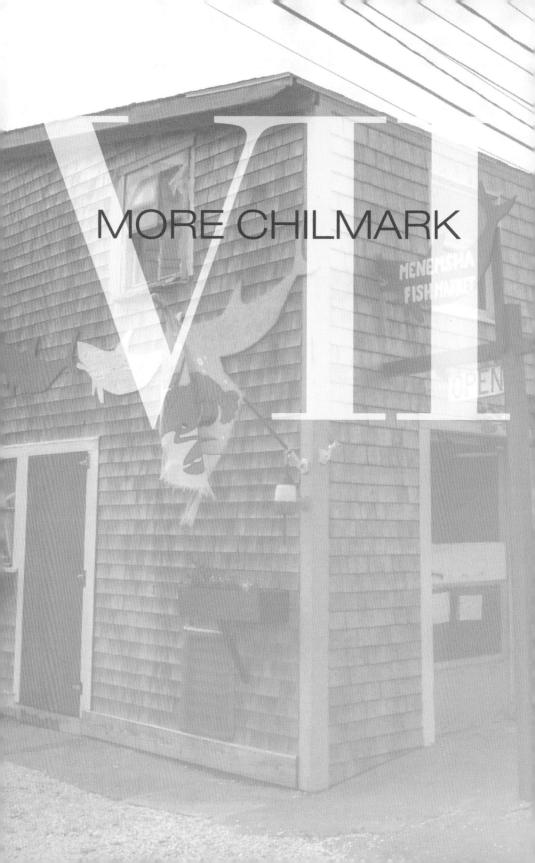

MORE CHILMARK

GPS: GPS: 41.349962, -70.791145

Directions from Previous Site: From the Vanderhoop Homestead, head back out on State Road and follow it 1.8 miles, then turn left onto Lobsterville Road. Follow it 1.1 miles to the next destination on the left. (Distance: 3 miles; Driving Time: 8 mins.)

1. LOBSTERVILLE BEACH
Lobsterville Road, Chilmark

This is a beautiful two-mile stretch of beach on the north side of Chilmark, but there's a catch: It is a public beach but parking on Lobsterville Road is not allowed. You'll need to find another spot to leave your vehicle before enjoying this gem. The beach stretches east to Menemsha Creek. As one would guess, Lobsterville got its name from lobstermen who spent summers fishing for the creatures in the area beginning in the 1870s. It became a deserted area when the lobstermen began to bring their boats to the safer area of Menemsha. Summer homes that have been built in the area have helped to restore Lobsterville as a getaway destination.

MORE CHILMARK

GPS: 41.351935, -70.767649

Directions from Previous Site: From Lobsterville Beach, continue on Lobsterville Road, and after 0.4 miles bear left onto West Basin Road. Follow it to the end and the next destination. (Distance: 1.4 miles; Driving Time: 4 mins.)

2. WEST BASIN & MENEMSHA BIKE FERRY
West Basin Road, Chilmark

Just across the creek from Menemsha is this popular fishing spot. There is a boat ramp for launching a vessel into the safe waters of a cove along Menemsha Creek before heading out into Vineyard Sound. This spot contains more than just the allure of fishing, however.

This is also the location of the Menemsha Bike Ferry. It is very convenient and unique,

turning what would be a nearly eight-and-a-half-mile journey around Menemsha Pond into a quick jump across the creek, saving lots of time and energy for bicyclists. It runs daily from 9 to 5 in the summer and on weekends in May.

Nestled in the beach grass along the creek is a plaque placed by the African American Heritage Trail of Martha's Vineyard. It honors the Wampanoag Tribe of Aquinnah for their bravery in disobeying the Fugitive Slave Act of 1850 by harboring runaway slaves on their journey to freedom. It is a powerful connection to the country's history in a spot one would not expect.

THE AFRICAN-AMERICAN HERITAGE
TRAIL OF MARTHA'S VINEYARD
HONORS THE WAMPANOAG TRIBE

"HE HAD RESOLVED WHEN HE RAN AWAY THE SECOND
TIME THAT HE WOULD NEVER BE TAKEN BACK ALIVE
BUT INSTEAD WOULD DIE FIGHTING FOR HIS FREEDOM."
NETTA VANDERHOOP, 3RD FEBRUARY, 1921

IN 1850 THE FEDERAL FUGITIVE SLAVE ACT REQUIRED THAT
PEOPLE RUNNING FROM SLAVERY IN THE SOUTH TO FREEDOM IN
THE NORTH MUST BE RETURNED TO THE SLAVEHOLDERS. TO HELP
A RUNAWAY ESCAPE WAS A CRIME.
THE WAMPANOAG TRIBE OF AQUINNAH DISOBEYED THE FUGITIVE
SLAVE ACT AND PROVIDED A REFUGE FOR RUNAWAYS HELPING THEM
ON THEIR ROAD TO FREEDOM.

RANDALL BURTON
EDGAR JONES

VIII

MORE WEST TISBURY

Directions from Previous Site: From the West Basin head back on West Basin Road, continue onto Lobsterville Road, turn left onto State Road. Follow it 4.2 miles, then turn right onto South Road. In 4.8 miles the road name changes back to State Road. In one-half mile bear right onto Edgartown/W. Tisbury Road. The next destination is a few hundred feet up on the right. (Distance: 12.1 miles; Driving Time: 29 mins.)

1. THE OLD MILL

690 Edgartown-West Tisbury Road, West Tisbury

Since the mid-seventeenth century this spot has been a site for industrial use. Mill Pond just across the street flows over a dam into a creek that runs parallel to the current mill structure. This was built in 1848 and is situated at the forefront of twenty-six acres, most of which lie behind the building. Across the street, the pond is usually filled with ducks and swans. There are benches so you can sit and enjoy their company. The fowl will congregate around you, hoping to be fed.

It was the first European settlers who dammed Mill Brook upon arrival on the island. The mill ceased operation just before the turn of the twentieth century. It is now owned by the Martha's Vineyard Garden Club. There is a small dirt parking area behind the building.

IX

EDGARTOWN

1. MANUEL F. CORRELLUS STATE FOREST

Barnes Road, Edgartown

Relax and take your time, you might be here for a while. The Correllus State Forest encompasses more than 5,300 acres in the middle of the island. You could spend hours traversing its pathways and only scratch the surface. There are more than fourteen miles of bike paths lining the forest, leading all across the Great Plain of the Vineyard. The forest was originally created in 1908 as a way to try to protect the heath hen. This bird was overhunted in the late nineteenth century, and in fact the last of the species were located on the Vineyard. It was last reported seen in 1932.

The forest is named after Manuel F. Correllus, the park superintendant for fifty-eight years until 1987. This land, which once nobody wanted, is now a pristine wilderness. It is hard to imagine that such a large forest exists on an island known for seemingly infinite stretches of beaches. This spot is well worth the time to stop and take a deep breath and enjoy the sights and scents of a forest only minutes from the ocean.

GPS: 41.349303, -70.511915

Directions from Previous Site: From Correllus State Forest, head south on Barnes Road, then turn left onto W. Tisbury Road. Follow it 4.2 miles, then turn right onto Robinson's Road. After 0.3 miles, turn right onto Peases Point Way S. (the road name changes to Katama Road). Follow it 3 miles to the end and the next destination. (Distance: 8.9 miles; Driving Time: 18 mins.)

2. KATAMA BEACH (SOUTH BEACH)

Atlantic Drive, Edgartown

A three-mile barrier beach along the south coast used to extend all the way to Chappaquiddick before a storm caused a breach in the shore in 2007. Katama is a village of Edgartown; Katama means "crab fishing place" in Wampanoag. This is a tremendously popular beach both for families and young adults who enjoy the heavy surf. The beach begins in the west at Edgartown Great Pond and continues to the east along Katama Bay to the breach in the shore. It is a large beach and although there are restrooms and lifeguards, not all sections of the beach have close access to these.

3. NORTON POINT BEACH
Katama Road, Edgartown

Steps from Katama Beach is Norton Point. This is the only beach on the island that allows off-road driving. Norton Point is still a barrier beach. Thanks to a storm in 2007, it developed a breach that broke the connection between Edgartown and Chappaquiddick. The currents are very powerful here and swimming or even wading into the water is strongly discouraged. As of April 2015, the breach between Norton Point and Wasque on Chappaquiddick had been reconnected and off-road travel had been permitted across the newly re-formed beach.

This is a beautiful spot and is relatively secluded though only a few hundred feet from

Wasque. The reconnection of the beach will certainly cause the amount of off-road travel to be in flux. It is best to check before heading out. As of 2015, off-road permits are $90 for island residents, $140 for off-island residents.

GPS: 41.389579, -70.510221

Directions from Previous Site: From Norton Point, head north on Katama Road, and follow it 2.7 miles then bear right onto Main Street. Follow it one-half mile, then bear left onto N. Water Street, and take the second right onto Dagget Street and the next destination. (Distance: 3.6 miles; Driving Time: 9 mins.)

4. CHAPPY FERRY

Dagget Street, Edgartown

Chappaquiddick sits only 527 feet from Edgartown, so close and yet so far. Chappaquiddick is not officially an island, although a breach at Norton Point during a storm in 2007 did cause it to be a true island temporarily until the beach was reconnected in March 2015. The easiest way to get to Chappaquiddick is by ferry; the ride across is barely two minutes and usually three vehicles and a handful of people can ride the barge-like *On Time II* or *On Time III* from shore to shore. If taking a ferry to the Vineyard is a vacation, then is taking the ferry across to Chappy a vacation within a vacation?

As of 2015 ferry rates are: $4 round-trip for passenger; $6 passenger with a bike; $12 passenger with a vehicle.

X
CHAPPAQUIDDICK ISLAND

GPS: 41.390452, -70.477954)

Directions from Previous Site: From the ferry, head east on Chappaquiddick Road for 1.4 miles, then turn left onto North Neck Road. Follow it 0.8 miles to the next destination on the right. (Distance: 2.2 miles; Driving Time: 16 mins.)

1. ROYAL & ANCIENT CHAPPAQUIDDICK LINKS

35 North Neck Road, Chappaquiddick

Nestled in the quiet solitude along North Neck Road is this historic gem. The Royal and Ancient Links is a golf course originally built and established in 1887, making it one of the oldest golf courses in the country. Though at one point it had twenty-four holes, it is currently only a nine-hole course. It is a slice of heaven for golfers among the scenery of Chappaquiddick. The tee markers are conch shells and the ocean is never more than a few hundred feet away. It is an out-of-the-way beauty that can be enjoyed by both golfer and non-golfer alike.

GPS: 41.396184, -70.469246

Directions from Previous Site: From the golf course, continue along North Neck Road 0.7 miles to the next destination on the left. (Distance: 0.7 miles; Driving Time: 5 mins.)

2. NORTH NECK HIGHLANDS PRESERVE

North Neck Road, Chappaquiddick

A long dirt road should not stop you from visiting this secluded but spectacular piece of Chappaquiddick. Traveling down North Neck Road for over a mile you come to a sign on the left that says "Cape Poge Gut Lot." There is a seashell-lined trail that leads you over thirty-five feet above the sea to overlook the tip of the Cape Poge Wildlife Refuge as well as much of the surrounding landscape. The view is simply breathtaking.

People come to this out-of-the-way location to fish, relax on the small beach, or even take a boat across to the Wildlife Refuge to find an even more secluded patch of sand. The powerful currents pushing through the Gut make it a great fishing spot but dangerous for swimming.

GPS: 41.375382, -70.458111

Directions from Previous Site: From North Neck, head back out on North Neck Road, turn left onto Chappaquiddick Road and follow it 1 mile, keep straight as it becomes Dyke Road. Continue 0.4 miles to the next destination on the left. (Distance: 2.9 miles; Driving Time: 21 mins.)

3. MYTOI GARDENS
56 Dike Road, Chappaquiddick

A Japanese-style garden might be one of the last things one would expect to see on the Vineyard, however, this is one of the most spectacular sites on the island. Designed by Edgartown resident Hugh Jones during the late 1950s, Mytoi became protected land as part of The Trustees of Reservations collection in 1976. The trails around the garden are only one-half mile, making it an easy walk and all the more enjoyable. Ironically the word "Mytoi" has no Japanese translation; Mr. Jones simply changed the spelling of "my toy," as that is how he often referred to his garden.

This is a definite must-see and although it might not be the first spot on your Chappy destination list, it might be the most unforgettable.

GPS: 41.373307, -70.452319

Directions from Previous Site: From Mytoi, continue east on Dyke Road for 0.3 miles, over the Dyke Road Bridge to the next destination. (Distance: 0.3 miles; Driving Time: 3 mins.)

4. CAPE POGE WILDLIFE REFUGE

Dike Road, Chappaquiddick

Part of nearly 1,000 acres of preserved land, this is the untouched beauty that many desire but rarely find. On the eastern half of Chappy, this area is also under the care of The Trustees of Reservations, the oldest statewide land conservation organization in the country, tracing its roots back to Charles Eliot in 1891.

Cape Poge Wildlife Refuge includes a seven-mile long barrier beach that curves around like a bent finger nearly retouching the land at the Cape Poge Gut. This refuge is a great area for shellfishing, specifically scalloping. Cape Poge likely got its name from the Algonquin word "capoak," meaning "heaven, cove."

There are a few homes along the Refuge that date back to before the land went into conservation. The refuge is home to what seems like unlimited numbers of shorebirds and small animals like deer. The dunes and ponds and water bodies like Shear Pin Pond and Cape Poge Bay can be explored by off-road vehicles with a permit, or even better by taking a guided tour through the Trustees. Either way this is the ultimate spot for peace and solitude on the Vineyard.

Directions from Previous Site: From the entrance to Cape Poge, begin heading north. This route is off-road and requires a permit or taking a group tour with the Trustees. The route to the next destination is approximately 3.3 miles. (Distance: 3.3 miles; Driving Time: Appx. 30 mins.)

5. CAPE POGE LIGHTHOUSE

Lighthouse Road, Chappaquiddick

The crown jewel of the Cape Poge Wildlife refuge is this beacon. Nearly five miles north of the Dike Bridge, out on the sand stands this lighthouse built in 1893. It is the third light erected on the spot; the previous two (built in 1801 and 1844, respectively) fell victim to the stormy sea. From the top of this structure, it is possible to see all the way to the shores of Nantucket eighteen miles away.

The foundation of the former lighthouse and keepers quarters can be seen just north of the present-day lighthouse along the immediate shore. Recent storms have eroded the dunes so that the brick and concrete is exposed. The lighthouse stands a total of sixty-three feet above sea level with its light visible up to nine miles at sea. One of the most remote lighthouses in the country, it stands as a connection to civilization in an area where there are few.

GPS: 41.352412, -70.463040)

Directions from Previous Site: From Cape Poge Lighthouse, head back south over the sand to Dyke Road. Follow it 0.8 miles, then bear left onto Chappaquiddick Road. Turn left onto Pocha Road and keep straight as it becomes Tackanash Road, then keep straight, bearing right onto Wasque Road. Turn right onto Trustees Lane and follow it to the next destination. (Distance: 6.7 miles; Driving Time: 58 mins.)

6. WASQUE
Wasque Road, Chappaquiddick

Somewhat of a hidden gem, Wasque is a 200-acre preserve of sand and trails. It is consistently rated as one of the top beaches not only on the Vineyard but in New England. The name, pronounced "way-skwee," is purported to come from the Algonquin word "wannasque," meaning "the ending."

In the southeastern corner of Chappaquiddick, Wasque has undergone some serious erosion. In 2007, a large storm caused a breach at neighboring Norton Point Beach. However the beach has been reconnected, and with that Chappaquiddick is no longer a true island as people are allowed again to drive on the newly re-formed beach. It is every bit as beautiful as locals say. Enjoy the reconnection while it is there—one never knows when another storm may tear the fragile beach apart again.

GPS: 41.369138, -70.475504

Directions from Previous Site: From Wasque, head back north on Pocha Road for 0.9 miles to the next destination on the right where Pocha Road meets Chappaquiddick Road. (Distance: 1.7 miles; Driving Time: 13 mins.)

7. "BLOW YOUR BUGLE CORNER"
Pocha Road, Chappaquiddick

Heading back from Wasque, as you get to a three-way intersection, don't blink or you might miss this odd landmark. On the corner is a granite stone with the phrase "Blow Your Bugle" engraved on it. Locals will refer to this spot as "Blow Your Bugle Corner" rather than use the names of the roads. In fact, many roads on Chappy don't get called by their proper names— more likely, they're referred to by landmarks at the end of the roads. Not until a modern 911 system came into use did the official road names on Chappy become more prominently used.

XI

MORE EDGARTOWN

1. MEMORIAL WHARF
Dock Street, Edgartown

Just steps from the Chappy ferry sits Memorial Wharf. It is an open-air pavilion where people can fish protected from the elements. There is also a stairway leading to a rooftop upper deck with spectacular views of the harbor, Chappy Ferry, and Edgartown Lighthouse.

Directions from Previous Site: From the wharf head east on Morse Street, then turn left onto N. Summer Street. Follow it 0.2 miles, then turn left onto Main Street, bear left onto N. Water Street, and take the second right onto Kelley Street. The destination is on the left. (Distance: 0.5 miles; Driving Time: 3 mins.)

2. KELLEY HOUSE
23 Kelley Street, Edgartown

One of the oldest hotels in America with roots back to 1742, this is still a popular location to this day. The hotel was named after owners Elizabeth Kelley and her husband William who purchased the establishment in 1891. Near the water in Edgartown, the Kelley House has elegant rooms in four unique buildings: Chappy House, Garden House, Wheel House, and Court House. Another attraction is the Newes From America Pub found at the base of the Kelley House. This spot features American and British fare and is open to all, not just guests of the hotel.

GPS: 41.389191,-70.512461

Directions from Previous Site: From the Kelley House, take the first left onto Dock Street, continue onto Main Street, and the destination is on the left. (Distance: 500 feet; Driving Time: 1 min.)

3. THE WHARF RESTAURANT & PUB
3 Main Street, Edgartown

Originally opened in 1933 as The Edgartown Kafe, this is a terrific establishment where the locals gather. The restaurant is separate from the pub, where people can watch sporting events. There are large portions of American favorites and, of course, seafood. It is centrally located in Edgartown, making it an easy walk to most attractions. The Wharf has been run by the Coogan family since 2004, and they keep the emphasis on family dining.

GPS: 41.389671,-70.512192

Directions from Previous Site: From The Wharf, continue northwest on Main Street, then take the first right onto N. Water Street. The destination is a few hundred feet up on the right. (Distance: 500 feet; Driving Time: < 1min.)

4. MURDICK'S FUDGE
21 N. Water Street, Edgartown

This is a perfect excuse to indulge one's sweet tooth. Murdick's has been using the same recipe for their delicious fudge, peanut brittle, and chocolate nut clusters since 1887. There is no need to mess with success. (There are additional locations in Oak Bluffs and Vineyard Haven.) Their treats are made right on the premises in full view of passersby. Whether you want to treat yourself or buy someone a gift from the island, this is a great place to stop.

5. VINEYARD VINES
27 N. Water Street, Edgartown

What began as a small business founded by Shep and Ian Murray, two brothers who grew up in Connecticut and had grown tired of the daily grind in Manhattan, has become a wildly popular clothing line. The Edgartown shop, opened in 1998, is the original location. They started by selling only ties but the line has grown to include other staples like belts, shirts, shorts, bags, and other items for men, women, and children. As of 2015, Vineyard Vines has forty stores, eight outlets, and ninety-seven retailers. It is known for its pink whale logo and preppy clothing.

GPS: 41.392566, -70.506495

Directions from Previous Site: From Vineyard Vines, continue east on N. Water Street for 0.3 miles. The next destination is on the left. (Distance: 0.3 miles; Driving Time: 1 min.)

6. HARBOR VIEW HOTEL
131 N. Water Street, Edgartown

This is a beautiful hotel with an even more beautiful view. Harbor View sits facing Edgartown Harbor and Chappaquiddick. It has been a staple in the town since 1891, and within a few years it had developed a reputation as a perfect seasonal getaway. There are 114 rooms in three different buildings and such luxurious amenities as a heated pool and yoga classes. It is also quite popular for weddings.

GPS: 41.390904,-70.503066

Directions from Previous Site: From the Harbor View, the next destination is directly across the street.

7. EDGARTOWN LIGHTHOUSE
N. Water Street

This is an unbelievable spot. The lighthouse sits a few hundred feet from the road, right on the shore. It seems as though every step from the road to the lighthouse gives you a fresh and beautiful view of the lighthouse. Once at the foot of the lighthouse, there are views of the Chappy ferry on the right while behind you is the majestic Harbor View Hotel.

The current lighthouse was actually moved to Edgartown from Ipswich's Crane's Beach in 1881. Before that the original light station looked more like a house with a lantern on top of it. There are frequent tours of the lighthouse from Memorial Day through Columbus Day, providing stunning views of the surrounding harbor.

MORE EDGARTOWN

GPS: 41.390741, -70.515763

Directions from Previous Site: From the lighthouse, continue east on N. Water Street, then take the first left onto Thayer Street and then the first left onto Fuller Street. Follow it 0.2 miles, then turn right onto Cottage Street, then left onto Peases Point Way N. and follow it 0.3 miles, then turn left onto Peases Point Way S., and then take the first left onto Main Street. The next destination is immediately on the left. (Distance: 0.8 miles; Driving Time: 4 mins.)

8. DR. DANIEL FISHER HOUSE
99 Main Street, Edgartown

This house is just one of many historic spots along Edgartown's Main Street. The Federal style gives it a feel of a government building. It was built in 1840 for Dr. Fisher, who was also a wealthy whaling ship owner. By 1850 Dr. Daniel Fisher & Company was the single largest maritime-related industry on the island thanks to their production of whale oil and candles.

In addition to this house. two other spots on the island are named after Dr. Fisher: Fisher Pond on North Road in West Tisbury and Doctor Fisher Road in West Tisbury. Dr. Fisher had the road that bears his name built so wagons could transport the flour ground at his mills in West Tisbury. This Main Street home is part of the Martha's Vineyard Preservation Trust. It can be rented for weddings and holiday parties. Tours of the house are available from Memorial Day through Columbus Day.

9. THE VINCENT HOUSE MUSEUM
99 Main Street, Edgartown

The oldest house on the island, the Vincent House was erected in 1672. It was donated to the Martha's Vineyard Preservation Trust in 1977 and moved to its current location from where it initially stood along Great Pond a few miles southwest.

Original builder William Vincent was one of the first Puritan settlers who came to the island under the leadership of Gov. Thomas Mayhew. The house stayed in the Vincent family for more than 250 years before being sold in the mid-twentieth century.

GPS: 41.390573, -70.515265

Directions from Previous Site: From the Vincent House, the next destination is immediately on the left up Main Street.

10. OLD WHALING CHURCH
89 Main Street, Edgartown

A stoically beautiful piece of architecture complete with Greek-style columns, this church is a must-see attraction on Main Street. It was built by whaling captains in 1843 with a ninety-three foot-tall tower that rises above all other buildings. It was formerly a Methodist church but is now owned by the Martha's Vineyard Preservation Trust. It is a popular spot for weddings.

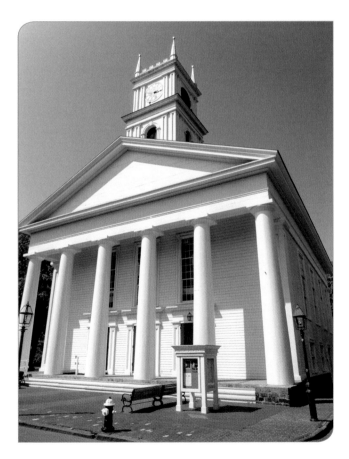

GPS: 41.389155, -70.514520

Directions from Previous Site: From the Whaling Church, head east down Main Street, take the second right onto S. Summer Street, and the next destination is a few hundred feet up on the right. (Distance: 0.1 miles; Driving Time: < 1min.)

11. THE CHARLOTTE INN
27 South Summer Street, Edgartown

Just a short walk from the bustle of Edgartown's Main Street is this Old World throwback. This inn combines elegance and seclusion with convenience. It has been lauded as a tremendous place to visit and stay by such publications as *Travel & Leisure* and *The New York Times*. The house itself dates back to 1866 and was at one time a grocery store. It was sold to Charlotte and Philip Pent in 1922, and in 1934 it became an inn named after Charlotte. The four buildings that make up the Charlotte Inn house seventeen charming individual rooms. It can be a home away from home for many travelers.

GPS: 41,388577, -70.516200

Directions from Previous Site: From the Charlotte Inn, continue south on S. Summer Street for 0.2 miles, then turn right onto High Street. Take the first right onto School Street, then follow it 0.2 miles to the next destination on the right. (Distance: .4 miles; Driving Time: 2 mins.)

12. MARTHA'S VINEYARD MUSEUM
59 School Street, Edgartown

A treat just away from the water in Edgartown, the Martha's Vineyard Museum has a great connection to the island's history. It was originally the Dukes County Historical Society, founded in 1922 when the collecting of island artifacts began. Miniature replicas of both Edgartown and Gay Head lighthouses sit in the grass outside the main museum building.

The museum houses historic coaches, boats, and surfboards inside the Carriage Shed as part of the permanent exhibitions. There are also temporary exhibitions featuring Vineyard history; see their website (Mvmuseum. org) for details. The museum provides a terrific look at the people and events that helped develop the island.

OAK BLUFFS

XIII

GPS: 41.416148, -70.548837

Directions from Previous Site: From the museum, continue north on School Street, take the first left onto Cooke Street and follow it for 0.4 miles. Then bear right onto Beach Road and continue 2.4 miles to the next destination on the right. (Distance: 3.2 miles; Driving Time: 8 mins.)

1. AMERICAN LEGION MEMORIAL BRIDGE (*JAWS* BRIDGE)
Edgartown-Oak Bluffs Road, Oak Bluffs

This bridge is the point where Edgartown becomes Oak Bluffs. The bridge has been renovated over the past several years. There are benches on either side of the bridge to enjoy the beauty of the Atlantic Ocean on one side, or Sengekontacket Pond on the other. However all of these facts pale in comparison as to why this run-of-the-mill bridge is so well known.

In 1975, the blockbuster movie *Jaws* was filmed on Martha's Vineyard and many of the locations shown in the film instantly became iconic. One such spot is this bridge. In the movie the shark enters the pond under the bridge and kills a man in a rowboat while several young boys watch in terror. It is hard to stand on the jetty looking back toward the bridge and not hear the chilling theme music in your mind. There are signs now that prohibit jumping off this bridge.

GPS: 41.422834, -70.553435

Directions from Previous Site: From the Jaws bridge, continue north on Beach Road for a half mile to next destination on the right. (Distance: 0.5 miles; Driving Time: 1 min.)

2. JOSEPH SYLVIA STATE BEACH
Beach Road, Oak Bluffs

This is a beautiful two-mile stretch of beach lying on the east coast of the Vineyard. There are no traditional parking lots but you can park along the road. These spots are almost always filled during the summer, so it is best to arrive early. This beach lies in both Edgartown and Oak Bluffs, but only the Oak Bluffs portion is called Joseph Sylvia Beach. As a state-owned beach it is free to all visitors. The waters here are calm, and it is a perfect beach for families.

This is also a barrier beach protecting Sengekontacket Pond. The pond's name likely comes from the Abnaki meaning "land at the mouth." This pond is alternately known as Anthiers Pond, which hearkens back to Gov. Thomas Mayhew's daughter Bethiah, who came to be known as Aunt Tiah, which developed into Anthiers.

GPS: 41.422604, -70.607737

Directions from Previous Site: From the bridge, head back south on Beach Road for 2.3 miles, then take a quick left onto Vineyard Haven Road. It becomes Edgartown/Vineyard Haven Road. Follow it a total of 4.2 miles, then at the rotary take the second exit. Follow it 0.3 miles to the next destination on the left. (Distance: 6.8 miles; Driving Time: 15 mins.)

3. ISLAND ALPACA COMPANY
Head of the Pond Road, Oak Bluffs

Here is a must-do family outing. At first glance, this looks to be a run-of-the-mill farm but that couldn't be further from the truth. The nineteen acres of land are home to a herd of sixty-nine Huacaya (wuh-kai-ya) alpacas and one llama. These adorable animals can be petted by children and adults alike and can also be purchased as pets. Huacaya alpacas are fluffy like a teddy bear. Their fiber is woven into beautiful garments that are for sale in the gift shop. Owner Barbara Ronchetti and her talented staff have run this highly successful business since 2004 when they owned a mere eight alpacas. Admission: $5

Directions from Previous Site: From Island Alpaca, head back to the rotary, then take the third exit onto Barnes Road. Follow it a total of 3.7 miles; the road name will change to Wing Road, then Circuit Avenue, then Samoset Avenue. Turn left onto Kennebec Avenue and follow it 0.2 miles, then turn right onto Lake Avenue and then left onto Seaview Avenue. Take the first right for the Steamship Authority. (Distance: 4.4 miles; Driving Time: 13 mins.)

4. LEAVING THE VINEYARD

Thank you for visiting Martha's Vineyard. I hope that you enjoyed your stay. Please come back anytime!

ACKNOWLEDGMENTS

Thank you to...

Mom & Dad, Kate, Lindsay, Ashley, Kaleigh, Emma, Liam, Landon, Lucas, Nina & Grampa, my aunts, uncles, and cousins too many to name.

Emily, Steve, Deanna & Michael, Meg, Judy, Rob, DJW, Mike & Barb's Bikes in Dennis, Monique, Maui, Debbie and the Clark Family

My good friend Bill DeSousa-Mauk, The Steamship Authority, and the great people at the Martha's Vineyard Chamber.

BIBLIOGRAPHY

Chappy Ferry website, http://chappyferry.com/.

Gay Head Lighthouse website, http://gayheadlight.org.

"Golf Course Details," The Royal and Ancient Chappaquiddick Links website, http://www. chappygolfclub.com/golf-course-info.

"Jaws," *Then & Now Movie Locations* (blog). "Jaws," entry August 16, 2013, http:// thennowmovielocations.blogspot.com/2014/08/jaws.html.

Knight, Margaret. "Chappy," *Vineyard Gazette*, Feb. 28, 2008. http://vineyardgazette.com/ news/2008/02/28/chappy?k=vg55805bfcaab09.

 "Martha's Vineyard," Steamship Authority website, https://www.steamshipauthority.com.

Martha's Vineyard Online website, http://mvol.com.t

New England Lighthouses: A Virtual Guide website, http://www.newenglandlighthouses.net.

Orner, Tony, "Despite Winter, Lagoon Pond Bridge on Schedule," *MV Times,* March 6, 2014, http://www.mvtimes.com/2014/03/06/despite-winter-slowdown-the-lagoon-pond-bridge-is-on-schedule.

Polly Hill Arboretum, http://www.pollyhillarboretum.org.

Schworm, Peter, "Vineyarders Want to Relocate Historic Historic Lighthouse," *The Boston Globe,* July 16, 2014, http://www.bostonglobe.com/metro/2014/07/16/martha-vineyard-town-moves-forward-with-plans-relocate-historic-lighthouse/iBTgvCb2jZZeYxKKFAUclJ/story.html.

Sistare, Heidi. "A River Runs Through It." *Martha's Vineyard* magazine, what was the original date of publication of the magazine, July 2014, http://www.mvmagazine.com/article.php?47409.

INDEX